MW00710529

The / Letters / of / Fabius, / in 1788, / on the Federal Constitution ; / .... / Copy-Right Secured. / From
the office of the Delaware / Gazette, Wilmington, / By
W. C. Smith. / 1797. /

8vo. pp. iv., 202 (1).

Written by John Dickinson, the " Pennsylvania Farmer,"
and member of the Annapolis and Philadelphia Conventions.
The Letters of Fabius were originally published in a Delaware
newspaper in 1788, and were not issued in pamphlet form till
1797, when they were reprinted as above, together with a
second series of letters " on the present situation of public
affairs," which are omited in this reprint. They were also included in " The Political Writings of John Dickinson,"
printed in 1801.

P. L. F.

THE EDITOR TO THE PUBLIC.

THE First Nine Letters in this Collection, published in the beginning of the Year 1788, were occasioned by an alarming hesitation of some States to ratify the Constitution proposed by the Federal Convention in 1787.

They appeared separately in News-papers; and have never been published together, before the present Edition.

Some Notes are added of Extracts from " *The Rights of Man*," published about three years after these Letters, containing similar sentiments, expressed with a remarkable resemblance of Language, especially on the two great subject—the *organization* of a *constitution* from original rights, and the *formation* of *government* from contributed rights, both of so much importance in laying regular *foundations* of Civil Society, and consequently in securing the advancement of *human happiness*.

LETTER I.

THE Constitution proposed by the Federal Convention now engages the fixed attention of America. .

Every person appears to be affected. Those who wish the adoption of the plan, consider its rejection as the source of endless contests, confusions, and misfortunes; and they also consider a resolution to alter, without previously adopting it, as a rejection.

Those who oppose the plan, are influenced by different views. Some of them are friends, others of them are enemies, to The United States. [2] The latter are of two classes; either men without principles or fortunes, who think they may have a chance to mend their circumstances, with impunity, under a weak government, or in public convulsions, but cannot make them worse even by the last—or men who have been always averse to the revolution; and though at first confounded by that event, yet, their hopes reviving with the declension of our affairs, have since persuaded themselves, that at length the people, tired out with their continued distresses, will return to their former connection with Great Britain. To argue with these opposers, would be vain—The other opposers of the plan deserve the highest respect.

What concerns all, should be considered by all; and individuals may injure a whole society, by not declaring their sentiments. It is therefore not only their right, but their duty, to declare them. Weak advocates of a good cause or artful advocates of a bad one, may endeavour to stop such communications, or to discredit them by clamour and calumny. This, however, is not the age for such tricks of controversy. Men have suffered so severely by being deceived upon subjects of the highest import, those of religion and freedom, that *truth* becomes infinitely valuable to them, not as a matter of curious speculation, but of beneficial practice—A spirit

of inquiry is excited, information diffused, judgment strengthened.

Before this tribunal of *the people*, let every one freely
speak, what he really thinks, [3] but with so sincere a reverence for the cause he ventures to discuss, as to use the utmost
caution, lest he should lead any into errors, upon a point of
such sacred concern as the public happiness.

It is not the design of this address, to describe the present
derangement of our affairs, the mischiefs that must ensue
from its continuance, the horrors, of a total dissolution of the
union, or of the division of it into partial confederacies. Nor
is it intended to describe the evils that will result from pur-
suing the plan of another Federal Convention; as if a better
temper of conciliation, or a more satisfactory harmony of decisions, could be expected from men, after their minds are
agitated with disgusts and disappointments, than before they
were thus disturbed; though from an uncontradicted assertion it appears, that without such provocations, the difficulty
of reconciling the interests of the several states was so near
to *insuperable,* in the late convention, that after many weeks
spent in the most faithful labours to promote concord, the
members were upon the very point of dispersing in the utmost
disorder, jealousy and resentment, and leaving the states exposed to all the tempests of passions, that have been so fatal
to confederacies of republics.

All these things, with observations on particular articles of
the constitution, have been laid before the public, and the
writer of this address means not to repeat what has been
already said. What he wishes, is to simplify [4] the subject,
so as to facilitate the inquiries of his fellow citizens.

Many are the objections made to the system proposed.
They should be distinguished. Some may be called local, because they spring from the supposed interests of individual
states. Thus, for instance, some inhabitants of large states
may desire the system to be so altered, that they may possess
more authority in the decisions of the government; or some
inhabitants of commercial states may desire it to be so altered, that the advantages of trade may center almost wholly

among themselves; and this predilection they may think com-
patible with the common welfare. Their judgment being thus
warp'd, at the beginning of their deliberations, objections are
accumulated as very important, that, without this preposses-
sion, would never have obtained their approbation. Certain
it is, that strong understandings may be so influenced by this
insulated patriotism, as to doubt—whether general benefits
can be communicated by a general government.*

Probably nothing would operate so much for the correction of these errors, as the perusal of the accounts transmitted to us by the ancients, of the calamities occasioned in
Greece by a conduct founded on similar mistakes. They are
expressly ascribed to this cause—that each city meditated a
part on its own profit and ends——insomuch that those *who
seemed to contend for union*, could never relinquish their own
in- [5] terests and advancement, while they deliberated for the
public.

Heaven grant! that our countrymen may pause in time—
duly estimate the present moment—and solemnly reflect—
whether their measures may not tend to draw down the same
distractions upon us, that desolated Greece.

They may now tolerably judge from the proceedings of
the Federal Convention and of other conventions, what are
the sentiments of America upon her present and future prospects. Let the voice of her distress be venerated—and ad-
hering to the generous Virginian declaration, let them resolve
to "*cling to Union as the political Rock of our Salvation.*"

FABIUS.

PHILADELPHIA, }
April 10, 1788. {

---

* See some late publications.

[6]   LETTER II.

But besides the objections originating from the before mentioned cause, that have been called local, there are other objections that are supposed to arise from maxims of liberty and policy.—

Hence it is inferred, that the proposed system has such inherent vices, as must necessarily produce a bad administration, and at length the oppression of a monarchy and aristocracy in the federal officers.

The writer of this address being convinced by as exact an investigation as he could make, that such mistakes may lead to the perdition of his country, esteems it his indispensable duty, strenuously to contend, that—*the power of the people* pervading the proposed system, together with the *strong confederation of the states*, forms an adequate security against every danger that has been apprehended.

If this single assertion can be supported by facts and arguments, there will be reason to hope, that anxieties will be removed from the minds of some citizens, who are truly devoted to the interests of America, and who have been thrown into perplexities, by the mazes of multiplied and intricate disquisitions.

The objectors agree, that the confederation of the states will be strong, according to the system proposed, and so strong, that many of them loudly complain of that strength. On this part of the assertion, there is no dispute: But some of the objections that have been published, [7] strike at another part of the principle assumed, and deny, that the system is sufficiently founded on the power of the people.

The course of regular inquiry demands, that these objections should be considered in the first place. If they are removed, then all the rest of the objections, concerning unnecessary taxations, standing armies, the abolishment of trial by jury, the liberty of the press, the freedom of commerce, the judicial, executive, and legislative authorities of the several states, and the rights of citizens, and the other abuses of federal government, must, of consequence, be rejected, if the principle contains the salutary, purifying, and preserving qualities attributed to it. The question then will be—not what may be done, when the government shall be turned into a tyranny; but how the government can be so turned?

Thus unembarrassed by subordinate discussions, we may come fairly to the contemplation of that superior point, and be better enabled to discover, whether our attention to it will afford any lights, whereby we may be conducted to peace, liberty, and safety.

The objections, denying that the system proposed is sufficiently founded on the power of the people, state, that the number of the federal trustees or officers, is too small, and that they are to hold their offices too long,

One would really have supposed, that smallness of number could not be termed a cause of danger, as influence must increase with enlargement. If this is a fault, it will soon be cor- [8] rected, as an addition will be often made to the number of the senators, and a much greater and more frequently, to that of the representatives; and in all probability much sooner, than we shall be able and willing to bear the expence of the addition.

As to the senate, it never can be, and it never ought to be large, if it is to possess the powers which almost all the objectors seem inclined to allot to it, as will be evident to every intelligent person, who considers those powers.

Though small, let it be remembered, that it is to be created by the sovereignties of the several states; that is, by the persons, whom the people of each state shall judge to be most worthy, and who, surely, will be religiously attentive to making a selection, in which the interest and honour of their state will be so deeply concerned. It should be remembered too, that this is the same manner, in which the members of Congress are now appointed; and that herein, the sovereignties of the states are so intimately involved, that however a renunciation of part of these powers may be desired by some of the states, it *never* will be obtained from the rest of them. Peaceable, fraternal, and benevolent as these are, they think, the concessions they have made, ought to satisfy all.

That the senate may always be kept full, without the interference of Congress, it is provided in the system, that if vacancies happen by resignation or otherwise, during the recess of the legislature of the state, the executive thereof may make temporary appointments, until the [9] next meeting of the legislature, which shall then fill up such vacancies.

As to the house of representatives, it is to consist of a number of persons, not exceeding one for every thirty thousand: But each state shall have at least one representative. The electors will reside, widely dispersed, over an extensive country. Cabal and corruption will be as impracticable, as, on such occasions, human institutions, can render them. The will of freemen, thus circumstanced, will give the fiat. The purity of election thus obtained, will amply compensate for the supposed defect of representation ; and the members, thus chosen, will be most apt to harmonize in their proceedings, with the general interests, feelings, and sentiments of the people.

Allowing such an increase of population as, from experience and a variety of causes, may be expected, the representatives, in a short period, will amount to several hundreds, and most probably long before any change of manners for the worse, that might tempt or encourage our ruler to mal-administration, will take place on this continent.

That this house may always be kept full, without the interference of Congress, it is provided in the system, that when vacancies happen in any state, the executive authority thereof shall issue writs of election to fill such vacancies.

But, it seems, the number of the federal officers is not only too small : They are to hold their offices too long.

[10] This objection surely applies not to the house of representatives, who are to be chosen every two years, especially if the extent of empire, and the vast variety and importance of their deliberations, be considered. In that view, they and the senate will actually be not only legislative but also diplomatic bodies, perpetually engaged in the arduous talk of reconciling, in their determinations, the interests of several sovereign states, not to insist on the necessity of a competent knowledge of foreign affairs, relative to the states.

They who desire the representatives to be chosen every year, should exceed Newton in calculations, if they attempt to evince, that the public business would, in that case, be better transacted, than when they are chosen every two years. The idea, however, should be excused for the zeal that prompted it.

Is monarchy or aristocracy to be produced, without the consent of the people, by a house of representatives, thus constituted?

It has been unanimously agreed by the friends of liberty, that *frequent elections of the representatives of the people, are the sovereign remedy of all grievances in a free government.*— Let us pass on to the senate.

At the end of two years after the first election, one third is to be elected for six years; and at the end of four years, another third. Thus one third will constantly have but four years, and another but two years to continue in office. The whole number at first will amount to [11] twenty-six, will be regularly renovated by the biennial election of one third, and will be overlooked, and overawed by the house of representatives, nearly three times more numerous at the beginning, rapidly and vastly augmenting, and more enabled to overlook and overawe them, by holding their offices for two years, as thereby they will acquire better information, respecting national affairs. These representatives will also command the public purse, as all bills for raising revenue, must originate in their house.

As in the Roman armies, when the Principes and Hastati had failed, there were still the Triarii, who generally put things to rights, so we shall be supplied with another resource.

We are to have a president, to superintend, and if he thinks the public weal requires it, to controul any act of the representatives and senate.

This president is to be chosen, not by the people at large, because it may not be possible, that all the freemen of the empire should always have the necessary information, for directing their choice of such an officer; nor by Congress, lest it should disturb the national councils; nor *by any one standing body whatever*, for fear of undue influence.

He is to be chosen in the following manner. Each state shall appoint, as the legislature thereof may direct, a number of electors, equal to the whole number of senators and representatives, to which the state shall be entitled in Congress: but no senator or representative, or person holding an office of trust or profit under the United States, shall be appointed an elector. As these elec- [12] tors are to be appointed, as the legislature of each state may direct, the fairest, freest opening is given, for each state to chuse such electors for this purpose, as shall be most signally qualified to fulfil the trust.

To guard against undue influence these electors, thus chosen, are to meet in their respective states, and vote by ballot; and still further to guard against it, Congress may determine the time of chusing the electors, and the days on which they shall give their votes—*which day shall be the same throughout the United States*. All the votes from the several states are to be transmitted to Congress, and therein counted. The president is to hold his office for four years.

When these electors meet in their respective states, utterly vain will be the unreasonable suggestions derived for partiality. The electors may throw away their votes, mark, with public disappointment, some person improperly favored by them, or justly revering the duties of their office, dedicate their votes to the best interests of their country.

This president will be no dictator. Two thirds of the representatives and the senate may pass any law, notwithstanding his dissent; and he is removable and punishable for misbehaviour.

Can this limited, fluctuating senate, placed amidst such powers, if it should become willing, ever become able, to make America pass under its yoke? The senators will generally be inhabitants of places very distant one from another. They can scarcely be acquainted till [13] they meet. Few of them can ever act together for any length of time, unless their good conduct recommends them to a re-election; and then there will be frequent changes in a body dependant upon the acts of other bodies, the legislatures of the several states, that are altering every year. Machiavel and Cæsar Borgia together could not form a conspiracy in such a senate, destructive to any but themselves and their accomplices.

It is essential to every good government, that there should be some council, permanent enough to get a due knowledge of affairs internal and external; so constituted, that by some deaths or removals, the current of information should not be impeded or disturbed; and so regulated, as to be responsible to, and controulable by the people. Where can the authority for combining these advantages, be more safely, beneficially, or satisfactorily lodged. than in the senate, to be formed according to the plan proposed? Shall parts of the trust be committed to the president, with counsellors who shall subscribe their advices?* If assaults upon liberty are to be guarded against, and surely they ought to be with sleepless vigilance, why should we depend more on the commander in chief of the army and navy of The United States, and of the militia of the several states, and on his counsellors, whom he may secretly influence, than of the senate to be appointed by the persons exercising the sovereign authority of the several states? In truth, the [14] objections against the powers of the senate originated from a desire to have them, or at least some of them, vested in a body, in which the several states should be represented, in proportion to the number of inhabitants, as in the house of representatives. This method is *unattainable*, and the wish for it should be dismissed from every mind, that desires the existence of a confederation.

What assurance can be given, or what probability be assigned, that a board of counsellors would continue honest, longer than the senate? Or, that they would possess more useful information, respecting all the states, than the senators of all the states? It appears needless to pursue this argument any further.

How varied, balanced, concordant, and benign, is the system proposed to us? To secure the freedom, and promote the happiness of these and future states, by giving *the will of the people* a decisive influence over the whole, and over all the

* See late publications.

parts, with what a comprehensive arrangement does it embrace different modes of representation, from an election by a county to an election by an empire? What are the complicated ballot, and all the refined devices of Venice for maintaining her aristocracy, when compared with this plain-dealing work for diffusing the blessings of equal liberty and common prosperity over myriads of the human race?

All the foundations before mentioned, of the federal government, are by the proposed system to be established, in the most clear, strong, [15] positive, unequivocal expressions, of which our language is capable. Magna charta, or any other law, never contained clauses more decisive and emphatic. While the people of these states have sense, they will understand them ; and while they have spirit, they will make them to be observed.

FABIUS.

---

[16]   LETTER III.

The writer of this address hopes, that he will now be thought so disengaged from the objections against the principle assumed, that he may be excused for recurring to his assertion, that—the power of the people pervading the proposed system, together with the strong confederation of the states, will form an adequate security against every danger that has been apprehended.

It is a mournful, but may be a useful truth, that the liberty of single republics has generally been destroyed by some of the citizens, and of confederated republics, by some of the associated states.

It is more pleasing, and may be more profitable to reflect, that, their tranquility and prosperity have commonly been promoted, in proportion to the strength of their government for protecting the worthy against the licentious.

As in forming a political society, each individual contributes some of his rights, in order that he may, from *a common stock* of rights, derive greater benefits, than he could from

merely *his own;* so, in forming a confederation, each political
society should contribute such a share of their rights, as will,
from *a common stock* of these rights, produce the largest quan-
tity of benefits for them.

But, what is that share? and, how to be managed? Momentous questions! Here, flattery is treason; and error,
destruction.

[17] Are they unanswerable? No. Our most gracious
Creator does not condemn us to sigh for unattainable blessed-
ness: But one thing he demands—that we should seek for
happiness in his way, and not in our own.

Humility and benevolence must take place of pride and
overweening selfishness. Reason, rising above these mists,
will then discover to us, that we cannot be true to ourselves,
without being true to others—that to love our neighbours as
ourselves, is to love ourselves in the best manner—that to give,
is to gain—and, that we never consult our own happiness
more effectually, than when we most endeavour to correspond
with *the divine designs,* by communicating happiness, as much
as we can, to our fellow-creatures. *Inestimable truth!* sufficient, if they do not barely ask what it is, to melt tyrants into
men, and to soothe the inflamed minds of a multitude into
mildness—*Inestimable truth!* which our Maker in his providence, enables us, not only to talk and write about, but to
adopt in practice of vast extent, and of instructive example.

Let us now enquire, if there be not some *principle,* simple
as the laws of nature in other instances, from which, as from
a *source,* the many benefits of society are deduced.

We may with reverence say, that our *Creator* designed
men for society, because otherwise they cannot be happy.
They cannot be happy without freedom; nor free without security; that is, without the absence of fear; nor thus secure,
without society. The con- [18] clusion is strictly syllogistic—
that men cannot be free without society. Of course, they
cannot be equally free without society, *which freedom produces the greatest happiness.*

As these premises are invincible, we have advanced a con-
siderable way in our enquiry upon *this deeply interesting sub-*

ject. If we can determine, what share of his rights, every individual must contribute to *the eommon stock* of rights in forming a society, for obtaining equal freedom, we determine at the same time, what share of their rights each political society must contribute to *the common stock* or rights in forming a confederation, which is only a larger society, for obtaining equal freedom : For, if the deposite be not proportioned to the magnitude of the association in the latter case, it will generate the same mischief among the component parts of it, from their inequality, that would result from a defective contribution to association in the former case, among the component parts of it, from their inequality.

Each individual then must contribute such a share of his rights, as is necessary for attaining that *security* that is essential to freedom ; and he is bound to make this contribution by the law of his nature, which prompts him to a participated happiness; that is, by the command of his creator ; therefore, he must submit his will, *in what concerns all*, to the will of all, that is of the whole society.   What does he lose by this submission ;   The power of doing [19] injuries to others—and the dread of suffering injuries from them.   What does he gain by it ?   The aid of those associated with him, for his relief from the incommodities of mental or bodily weakness—the pleasure for which his heart is formed—of doing good—*protection* against injuries—a capacity of enjoying his undelegated rights to the best advantage—a repeal of his fears—and tranquility of mind—or, in other words, that perfect liberty better described in the Holy Scriptures, than any where else, in these expressions—" When every man shall sit under his vine, and under his fig-tree, and *none shall make him afraid*."

The like submission, with a correspondent expansion and accommodation, must be made between states, for obtaining the like benefits in a confederation.   *Men* are the materials of both.   As the largest number is but a junction of *units*—a confederation is but an assemblage of individuals.   The auspicious influence of the law of his nature, upon which the happiness of *man* depends in society, must attend him in confederation, or he becomes unhappy ; for confederation should promote the happiness of individuals, or it does not *answer the intended purpose.* Herein there is a progression, not a contradiction. As *man*, he becomes a citizen ; as a citizen, he becomes a federalist. The generation of one, is not the destruction of the other. He carries into society his naked rights : These thereby improved, he carries still forward into confederation. If that sacred law before mentioned, is not here [20] observed, the confederation would not be real, but pretended. He would confide, and be deceived.*

* " The error of those who reason by precedent, drawn from antiquity, respecting the rights of man, is, that they do not go far enough into antiquity. They do not go the whole way. They stop in some of the intermediate stages of an hundred or a thousand years, and produce what was then done, as a rule for the present day. This is no authority at all. If we travel still further into antiquity, we shall find a direct contrary opinion and practice prevailing ; and if antiquity is to be authority, a thousand such authorities may be produced, successively contradicting each other : but if we proceed on, at last we shall come out right : We shall then come to the time when man came from the hand of his Maker. What was he then ? *Man.* Man was his high and only title, and a higher cannot be given him——We are now got at the origin of man, and at the origin of his rights.——Every history of the creation, and every traditionary account, whether from the lettered or unlettered world, however they may vary in their opinion or belief of certain particulars, all agree in establishing one point, the *unity* of man ; by which I mean that man is all of one degree, and consequently that all men are born equal, and with equal natural rights. By considering man in this light, it places him in a close connection with all his duties, whether to his *Creator*, or to the creation, of which he is a part ; and it is only where he forgets his *origin*, or, to use a more fashionable phrase, his birth and family, that he becomes dissolute.

" Hitherto we have spoken only (and that but in part) of the natural rights of man. We have now to consider the civil rights of man, and to shew how the one *originates* out of the other.—Man did not enter into society, to become worse than he was before, nor to have less rights than he had before, but to have those rights *better secured.* His natural rights are the foundation of all his civil rights. But in order to pursue this distinction with more precision, it will be necessary to mark the different qualities of natural and civil rights.

" A few words will explain this. Natural rights are those which appertain to man in the right of his existence—civil rights are those which appertain to man in right of his being a member of society. Every civil right has for its foundation some natural right pre-existing in the individual, but to unite his individual power is not, in all cases, sufficiently competent. Of this kind are all those which relate to *security* and *protection.*

" From this short review it will be easy to distinguish between that class of natural rights which man retains after entering into society, and those which

[21] The dilemma is inevitable. There must either be one will, or several wills. If but one will, all the people are concerned: if several wills, few comparatively are concerned. Surprizing! that this doctrine should be contended for by those, who declare, that the constitution is not founded on a bottom broad enough ; and, though *the whole people* of the United States are to be *trebly* represented in it in *three different modes* of representation, and their servants will have the most advantageous situations and opportunities of acquiring all requisite information for the welfare of the [22] whole union, yet insist for a privilege of opposing, obstructing, and confounding all their measures taken with common consent for the general weal, by the delays, negligences, rivalries, or other selfish views of parts of the union.

Thus, while one state should be relied upon by the union for giving aid, upon a recommendation of Congress, to another in distress, the latter might be ruined ; and the state relied upon, might suppose, it would gain by such an event.

When any persons speak of a consideration, do they, or do they not acknowledge, that the whole is interested in the safety of every part—in the agreement of parts—in the relation of parts [23] to one another—to the whole—or, to other societies? If they do—then, the authority of the whole, must be co-extensive with its interests—and if it is, the will of the whole must and ought in such cases to govern ; or else the whole would have interests without an authority to manage them—a position which prejudice itself cannot digest.

If they do not acknowledge, that the whole is thus interested, the conversation should cease. Such persons mean not a confederation, but something else.

---

he throws into *common stock* as a member of society. The natural rights which he retains, are all those in which the power to execute is as perfect in the individual as the right itself.—The natural rights which are not retained, are all those in which, though the right is perfect in the individual, the power to execute them is defective : *they answer not his purpose*—those he *deposits* in the *common stock* of society, and takes the arm of society, of which he is a part, in preference and in addition to his own. Society grants him nothing. Every man is a proprietor in society, and draws on the capital as a matter of right."— "*Rights of Man*," 1791, page 30, 31.

As to the idea, that this superintending sovereign will must of consequence destroy the subordinate sovereignties of the several states, it is begging a concession of the question, by inferring, that a manifest and great usefulness must necessarily end in abuse ; and not only so, but it requires an extinction of the principle of all society: for the subordinate sovereignties, or, in other words, the undelegated rights of the several states, in a confederation, stand upon the very same foundation with the undelegated rights of individuals in a society, the federal sovereign will being composed of the subordinate sovereign wills of the several confederated states. As some persons seem to think, a bill of rights is the best security of rights, the sovereignties of the several states have this best security by the proposed constitution, and more than this best security, for they are not barely declared to be rights, but are taken into it as component parts for their perpetual preservation—by themselves. In short, the government of each state is, and is to be, [24] sovereign and supreme in all matters that relate to each state only. It is to be subordinate barely in those matters that relate to the whole ; and it will be their *own faults* if the several states suffer the federal sovereignty to interfere in things of their respective jurisdictions. An instance of such interference with regard to any single state, will be a dangerous precedent as to all, and therefore will be guarded against by all, as the trustees or servants of the several states will not dare, if they retain their senses, so to violate the independent sovereignty of their respective states, *that justly darling object* of American affections, to which they are responsible, besides being endeared by all the charities of life.

The common sense of mankind agrees to the devolutions of individual wills in society ; and if it has not been as universally assented to in confederation, the reasons are evident, and worthy of being retained in remembrance by Americans. They were want of opportunities, or the loss of them, through defects of knowledge and virtue. The principle, however, has been sufficiently vindicated in imperfect combinations, as their prosperity has generally been commensurate to its operation.

How beautifully and forcibly does the inspired Apostle Paul, argue upon a sublimer subject, with a train of reasoning strictly applicable to the present? His words are—"If the foot shall say, because I am not the hand, I am not of the body; is it therefore not of the body? and if the ear shall say, because I am [25] not the eye, I am not of the body; is it therefore not of the body?" As plainly inferring, as could be done in that allegorical manner, the strongest censure of such partial discontents and dissentions, especially, as his meaning is enforced by his description of the benefits of union in these expressions—" But, now they are many members, yet but one body : and·the eye *cannot* say to the hand, I have no need of thee."

When the commons of Rome upon a rupture with the Senate, seceded in arms at the Mons sacer, Menemius Agrippa used the like allusion to the human body, in his famous apologue of a quarrel among some of the members. The unpolished but honest-hearted Romans of that day, understood him, and were appeased.

Another comparison has been made by the learned, between a natural and a political body ; and no wonder indeed, when the title of the latter was borrowed from the resemblance. It has therefore been justly observed, that if a mortification takes place in one or some of the limbs, and the rest of the body is sound, remedies may be applied, and not only the contagion prevented from spreading, but the diseased part or parts saved by the connection with the body, and restored to former usefulness. When general putrefaction prevails, death is to be expected. History sacred and profane tells us, that, *corruption of manners sinks nations into slavery.*

FABIUS.

[26]   LETTER IV.

Another question remains.   How are the contributed rights to be managed?   The resolution has been in great measure anticipated, by what has been said concerning the system proposed.   Some few reflections may perhaps finish it.

If it be considered separately, a *constitution* is the *organization* of the contributed rights in society.   *Government* is the *exercise* of them.   It is intended for the benefit of the governed ; of course can have no just powers but what conduce to that end : and the awfulness of the trust is demonstrated in this—that it is founded on the nature of man, that is, on the will of his *Maker*, and is therefore˙ sacred.   It is then an offence against Heaven, to violate that trust.*

[27] If the organization of a constitution be defective, it may be amended,

A good constitution promotes, but not always produces a good administration.

* " We have now traced Man from a natural individual to a member of society——Civil power, properly considered as such is made up of the *aggregate* of that class of the natural rights, which become defective in the individual in point of power, and *answers not his purpose ;* but when collected into a focus, becomes competent to the purpose of every one.——Let us now apply those principles to government,——

" Individuals themselves, each in his own personal and sovereign right, entered into a compact with each other, to produce a government ; and this is the only mode in which governments have a right to arise, and the only principle on which they have a right to exist.

" A *constitution* is not a thing in name only, but in fact.—It has not an ideal but a real existence, and wherever it cannot be produced in a visible form, there is none.   A *constitution* is a thing antecedent to a *government ;* and a government is only the creature of a constitution.—A constitution of a country is not the act of its government, but of the people constituting a government. It is the body of elements to which you can refer, and quote article by article ; and which contains the principles on which the government shall be established, the manner in which it shall be organized, the powers it shall have, the mode of election, the duration of parliaments, or by what other name such bodies may be called, the powers which the executive part of the government shall have ; and, in fine, every thing that relates to the complete *organization* of a civil government, and the principles on which it shall act, and by which it shall be bound."—" *Rights of Man,*" page 35, 36.

The government must never be lodged in a single body. From such an one, with an unlucky composition of its parts, rash, partial, illegal, and when intoxicated with success, even cruel, insolent and contemptible edits, may at times be expected. By these, if other mischiefs do not follow, the national dignity may be impaired.

[28] Several inconveniences might attend a division of the government into two bodies, that probably would be avoided in another arrangement.

The judgment of the most enlightened among mankind, confirmed by multiplied experiments, points out the propriety of government being committed to such a number of great departments, as can be introduced without confusion, distinct in office, and yet connected in operation. It seems to be agreed, that three or four of these departments are a competent number.

[29] Such a repartition appears well calculated to express the sense of the people, and to encrease the safety and repose of the governed, which with the advancement of their happiness in other respects, are the objects of government ; as thereby there will be more obstructions interposed ; against errors, feuds, and frauds, in the administration, and the extraordinary interference of the people need be less frequent. Thus, wars, tumults, and uneasinesses, are avoided. The departments so constituted, may therefore be said to be balanced.

But, notwithstanding, it must be granted, that a bad admin-

"What is a constitution ? it is the form of government, delineated by the mighty hand of the people, in which certain first principles or fundamental laws are established. The constitution is certain and fixed ; it contains the permanent will of the people, and is the supreme law of the land ; it is paramount to the power of the legislature, and can be revoked or altered only by the authority that made it.—What are legislatures ? creatures of the constitution, they owe their existence to the constitution—they derive their powers from the constitution.—It is their commission, and therefore all their acts must be conformable to it, or else void. The *constitution* is the work or will of the *people themselves*, in their original, sovereign, and unlimited capacity. Law is the work or will of the legislature in their derivative capacity."

Judge Patterson's charge to the Jury in the Wioming case of Vanhorne's lessee against Dorrance ; tried at the circuit-court for the United States, held at Philadelphia, April term, 1795.

istration may take place.—What is then to be done? The
answer is instantly found—Let the Fasces be lowered before
—the supreme sovereignty of the people. *It is their duty to
watch, and their right to take care, that the constitution be preserved;* or in the Roman phrase on perilous occasions—*to pro-
vide, that the republic receive no damage.*

Political bodies are properly said to be balanced, with respect to this *primary origination* and *ultimate destination*, not
to any intrinsic or constitutional properties.* It [30] is the
power from which they *proceed,* and which they *serve,* that
truly and of right balances them.†

But, as a good constitution not always produces a good
administration, a defective one not always excludes it. Thus
in governments very different from those of United America,
general manners and customs, improvement in knowledge,
and the education and disposition of princes, not unfrequently soften the features, [31] and qualify the defects.
Jewels of value are substituted, in the place of the rare
and genuine orient of higest price and brightest lustre :
and though the sovereigns cannot even in their ministers, be
brought to account by the governed, yet there are instances
of their conduct indicating a veneration for the rights of the

* Constitutional properties are only, as has been observed at the beginning
of this letter, parts in the organization of the contributed rights. As long as
those parts preserve the orders assigned to them respectively by the constitution, they may so far be said to be balanced : but, when one part, without
being sufficiently checked by the rest, abuses its power to the manifest
danger of public happiness, or when the several parts abuse their respective
powers so as to involve the commonwealth in the like peril, *the people* must
restore things to that order, from which their functionaries have departed. If
the people suffer this living principle of watchfulness and controul to be extin-
guished among them, they will assuredly not long afterwards experience that
of their "temple," "there shall not be left one stone upon another, that shall
not be thrown down."

† When the *controuling power* is in a constitution, it has the *nation* for its
support, and the *natural* and the political controuling powers are together.
The laws which are enacted by the governments, controul men only as
individuals, but the *nation*, thro' its constitution controuls *the whole government*, and has a *natural ability* to do so. The *final controuling* power, therefore, and the *original constituting* power, *are one and the same power.*—" *Rights
of Man,*" 1792, part 2d, b. 4, page 42.

people, and an internal conviction of the guilt that attends their violation. Some of them appear to be fathers of their countries. Revered princes! Friends of mankind! May peace be in their lives—and in their deaths—Hope.

By this superior will of the people, is meant a reasonable, not a distracted will. When frenzy seizes the mass, it would be equal madness to think of their happiness, that is, of their freedom. They will infallibly have a Philip or a Cæsar, to bleed them into soberness of mind. At present we are cool; and let us attend to our business.

Our goverment under the proposed confederation, will be guarded by a repetition of the strongest cautions against excesses. In the senate the sovereignties of the several states will be equally represented; in the house of representatives, the people of the whole union will be equally represented; and, in the president, and the federal independent judges, so much concerned in the execution of the laws, and in the determination of their constitutionality, the sovereignties of the several states and the people of the whole union, may be considered as conjointly represented.

[32] Where was there ever and where is there now upon the face of the earth, a government so diversified and attempered? If a work formed with so much deliberation, so respectful and affectionate an attention to the interests, feelings, and sentiments of all United America, will not satisfy, what would satisfy all United America?

It seems highly probable, that those who would reject this labour of public love, would also have rejected the Heaven-taught institution of *trial by jury*, had they been consulted upon its establishment. Would they not have cried out, that there never was framed so detestable, so paltry, and so tyrannical a device for extinguishing freedom, and throwing unbounded domination into the hands of the king and barons, under a contemptible pretence of preserving it? " What! Can freedom be preserved by imprisoning its guardians? Can freedom be preserved, by keeping twelve men closely confined without meat, drink, fire, or candle, until they unanimously agree, and this to be innumerably repeated? Can freedom be preserved, by thus delivering up a number of freemen to a monarch and an aristocracy, fortified by dependant and obedient judges and officers, to be shut up, until under duress they speak as they are ordered? Why cannot the twelve jurors separate,* after hearing the evidence, return to their respective homes, and there take time,* and think of the matter at their ease?* Is there not a variety of [33] ways, in which causes have been, and can be tried, without this *tremendous, unprecedented inquisition?* Why then is it insisted on; but because the fabricators of it know that it will, and intend that it shall reduce the people to slavery? Away with it—Freemen will never be enthralled by so insolent, so execrable, so pitiful a contrivance."

Happily for us our ancestors thought otherwise. They were not so over-nice and curious, as to refuse blessings, because, they might possibly be abused.

They perceived, that the uses included were great and manifest. Perhaps they did not foresee, that from this acorn, as it were, of their planting, would be produced a perpetual vegetation of political energies, that "would secure the just liberties of the nation for a long succession of ages,* and elevate it to the distinguished rank it has for several centuries held. As to abuses, they trusted to their own spirit for preventing or correcting them: And worthy is it of deep consideration by every friend of freedom, that abuses that seem to be but "trifles,"† may be attended by fatal consequences. What can be "trifling," that diminishes or detracts from the only defence, that ever was found against "open attacks and secret machinations?"‡ This establishment originates from a knowledge of human nature. With a superior force, wisdom, and benevolence uni- [34] ted, it rives the difficulties concerning administration of justice, that have distressed, or destroyed the rest of mankind. It reconciles contradictions—vastness of power, with safety of private station. It is ever new, and always the same.

---

* See late publications against the Federal Constitution.

* Blackstone, III. 279   † Idem, IV. 350.   ‡ Idem, III. 381.

Trial by jury and the dependence of taxation upon representation, those corner stones of liberty, were not obtained by a bill of rights, or any other records, and have not been and cannot be preserved by them. They and all other rights must be preserved, by *soundness of sense and honesty of heart.* Compared with these, what are a bill of rights, or any characters drawn upon paper or parchment, those frail remembrances? Do we want to be reminded, that the sun enlightens, warms, invigorates, and cheers? or how horrid it would be, to have his blessed beams intercepted, by our being thrust into mines or dungeons? Liberty is the sun of society. Rights are the beams.*

[35] "It is the duty which every man owes to his country, his friends, his posterity, and himself, to maintain to the utmost of his power this valuable palladium in all its rights; to restore to its ancient dignity, if at all impaired by the different value of property, or otherwise deviated from its first institution; to amend it, wherever it is defective;* and above all to guard with the most jealous circumspection against the new and arbitrary methods of trial, which, under a variety of plausible pretences, may in time imperceptibly undermine this best preservative of liberty."† Trial by Jury is our birth-right; and tempted to his own ruin, by some seducing spirit, must be the man, who in opposition to the genius of United America, shall dare to attempt its subversion.

In the proposed confederation, it is preserved inviolable in criminal cases, and cannot be altered in other respects, but when United America demands it.

There seems to be a disposition in men to find fault, no dif-

---

* Instead of referring to musty records and mouldy parchments to prove that the rights of the living are lost, "renounced, and abdicated for ever," by those who are now no more. ——M. de la Fayette, in his address to the national assembly, applies to the living world, and says—"Call to mind the sentiments which nature has engraved in the heart of every citizen, and which take a new face when they are solemnly recognized by all. For a nation to love liberty, it is sufficient that she knows it ; and to be free, it is sufficient that she wills it,"—"*Rights of Man,*" page 11.

* See an enumeration of defects in trials by jury. Blackstone, III. 381.
† Idem, IV. 350.

ficult matter, rather than to act as they ought. The works of creation itself have been objected to: and one learned prince declared, that if he had been consulted, they would have been improved. With what book has so much fault been found, as with the Bible? Perhaps, principally, because it so clearly and strongly enjoins men *to do right.* How many, how plausible objections have been [36] made against it, with how much ardor, with how much pains? Yet, the book has done more good than all the books in the world; would do much more, if duly regarded; and might lead the objectors against it to happiness, if they would value it as they should.

When objections are made to a system of high import, should they not be weighed against the benefits? Are these great, positive, immediate? Is there a chance of endangering them by rejection or delay? *May they not be attained without admitting the objections at present,* supposing the objections to be well founded? If the objections are well founded, may they not be hereafter admitted, without danger, disgust, or inconvenience? Is the system so formed, that they may be thus admitted? May they not be of less efficiency, than they are thought to be by their authors? are they not designed to hinder evils, which are generally deemed to be sufficiently provided against? May not the admission of them prevent benefits, that might otherwise be obtained? In political affairs, is it not more safe and advantageous, for all to agree in measures that may not be best, than to quarrel among themselves, what are best?

When questions of this kind with regard to the plan proposed, are calmly considered, it seems reasonable to hope, that every faithful citizen of United America, will make up his mind, with much satisfaction to himself, and advantage to his country.

FABIUS.

LETTER V.

[37] It has been considered, what are the rights to be contributed, and how they are to be managed; and it has been said, that republican tranquility and prosperity have commonly been promoted, in proportion to the strength of governnment for protecting the worthy against the licentious.

The protection herein mentioned, refers to cases between citizens and citizens, or states and states: But there is also a protection to be afforded to all the citizens, or states, against foreigners. It has been asserted, that this protection never can be afforded, but under an appropriation, collection, and application, of the general force, by the will of the whole combination. This protection is in a degree dependent on the former, as it may be weakened by internal discords and especially where the worst party prevails. Hence it is evident, that such establishments as tend most to protect the worthy against the licentious, tends most to protect all against foreigners. This position is found to be verified by indisputable facts, from which it appears, that when nations have been, as it were, condemned for their crimes, unless they first became suicides, foreigners have acted as executioners.

This is not all. As government is intended for the happiness of the people, the protection of the worthy against those of contrary characters, is calculated to promote the end of legitimate government, that is the general welfare; [38] for *the government will partake of the qualities of those whose authority is prevalent.* If it be asked, who are the worthy, we may be informed by a heathen poet—

> "Vir bonus est quis?
> "Qui consulta patrum, qui leges juraque servat."*

The best foundations of this protection, that can be laid by man, are a constitution and government secured, as well as can be, from the undue influence of passions either in the people or their servants. Then in a contest between citizens and citizens, or states and states, the standard of laws may be displayed, explained and strengthened by the well-remembered

---

* He who reverses the constitution. liberties and laws of his country.——

sentiments ,and examples of our fore-fathers, which will give
it a sanctity far superior to that of their eagles so venerated
by the former masters of the world.   This circumstance will
carry powerful aids to the true friends of their country, and
unless counteracted by the follies of Pharsalia, or the acci-
dents of Philippi, may secure the blessings of freedom to
succeeding ages.

It has been contended that the plan proposed to us, adequately secures us against the influence of passions in the
federal servants.   Whether it as adequately secures us against
the influence of passions in the people, or in particular states,
time will determine, and *may the determination be propituous.*

[39] Let us now consider the tragical play of the passions
in similar cases; or, in other words, the consequences of their
irregularities.   Duly governed, they produce happiness.

Here the reader, is respectfully ¡requested, to assist the
intentions of the writer, by keeping in mind, the ideas of a
single republic with one democratic branch in its government,
and of a confederation of republics with .one or several democratic branches in the government of the confederation, or in
the government of its parts, so that as he proceeds, a comparison may easily run along, between any of these and the
proposed plan.

History is entertaining and instructive; but if admired
chiefly for amusement, it may yield little profit.   If read for
improvement, it is apprehended. a slight attention only will
be paid to the vast variety of particular incidents, unless they
be such as may meliorate the heart.   A knowledge of the
distinguishing features of nations, the principles of their governments, the advantages and disadvantages of their situations,
the methods employed to avail themselves of the first, and to
alleviate the last, their manners, customs, and institutions, the
sources of events, their progresses, and determining causes,
may be eminently useful, tho' obscurity may rest upon a
multitude of attending circumstances.   Thus one nation may
become prudent and happy, not only by the wisdom and success, but even by the errors and misfortunes of another.

[40] In Carthage and Rome, there was a very numerous

senate, strengthened by prodigious attachments, and in a great degree independent of the people. In Athens, there was a senate strongly supported by the powerful court of Arcopagus. In each of these republics, their affairs at length became convulsed, and their liberty was subverted. What cause produced these effects? Encroachments of the senate upon the authority of the people? No! but directly the reverse, according so the unanimous voice of historians; that is, encroachments of the people upon the authority of the senate. The people of these republics absolutely *laboured* for their own destruction; and never thought themselves so free, as when they were promoting their own subjugation. Though even after these encroachments had been made, and ruin was spreading around, yet the remnants of senatorial authority delayed the final catastrophe.*

[41] In more modern times, the Florentines exhibited a memorable example. They were divided into violent parties; and the prevailing one vested exorbitant powers in the house of Medici, then possessed, as it was judged, of more money than any crowned head in Europe. Though that house engaged and persevered in the attempt, yet the people were never despoiled of their liberty, until they were overwhelmed by the armies of foreign princes, to whose enterprizes their situation exposed them.

Republics of later date and various form have appeared. Their institutions consist of old errors tissued with hasty inventions, somewhat excusable, as the wills of the Romans, made with arms in their hands. Some of them were condensed†, by dangers. They are still compressed by them into

---

* The great Bacon, in enumerating the art by which Cæsar enslaved his country, says—"His first artifice was to break the strength of the senate, for while that remained safe, there was no opening for any person to immoderate or extraordinary power.——' *Nam initio sibi erani frangendæ senatus opes et autoritas qua salva nemini ad, immodica et extra ordinaria imperia aditus erat.*' Bossuet, bishop of Meaux, takes notice in his universal history, that the infamous Herod, to engross authority, attacked the Sanhedrim, which was in a manner the senate, where the supreme jurisdiction was exercised."

† "If we consider what the principles are that first condense man into society, and what the motive is that regulates their mutual intercourse afterwards, we shall find, by the time we arrive at what is called government, that nearly the whole of the business is performed by the natural operation of the parts upon each other."—*Rights of Man.*

a sort of union. Their well-known transactions witness, that their connection is not enough compact and arranged. They have all suffered, or are suffering through that defect. Their existence seems to depend more upon others, than upon themselves. There might be an impropriety in saying more, considering the peculiarity of their circumstances at this time.

[42] The wretched mistake of the great men who were leaders in the long parliament of England, in attempting, by not filling up vacancies, to extend their power over a brave and sensible people, accustomed to *popular representation*, and their downfal, when their victories and puissance by sea and land had thrown all Europe into astonishment and awe, shew, how difficult it is for rulers to usurp over a people who are not wanting to themselves.

Let the fortunes of confederated republics be now considered.

"The Amphictionic council," or "general court of Greece," claims the first regard. Its authority was very great : But, the parts were not sufficiently combined, to guard against the ambitious, avaricious, and selfish projects of some of them ; or, if they had the power, they dared not to employ it, as the turbulent states were very sturdy, and made a sort of partial confederacies.*

[43] "The Achæan league" seems to be the next in dignity. It was at first, small, consisting of few states : afterwards, very

---

* When Xerxes invaded Greece with the largest host and the greatest fleet that ever were collected, events occurred, which being preserved in history, convey to us a very affecting and instructive information.

While the danger was at some distance, the states of Greece looked to remote friends for assistance. Disappointed in these speculations, tho' the vast armaments of their enemies were constantly rolling towards them, still there was no firmness in their union, no vigor in their resolutions.

The Persian army passed the Hellespont, and directed its march westward. It was then decided, that Thessaly was the frontier to be first attacked.

The Thessalians, than whom no people had been more forward in the common cause, hastened a remonstrance to Corinth, urging that unless they were immediately and powerfully supported, necessity would oblige them to make terms with the invaders.

This reasonable remonstrance roused the sluggish and hesitating councils extensive, constituting of many. In their diet or Congress, they enacted laws, disposed of vacant employments, declared war, made peace, entered into alliances, compelled every state of the union to [44] obey its ordinances, and managed other affairs. Not only their laws, but their magistrates, council, judges, money, weights and measures, were the same. So uniform were they, that all seemed to be but one state. Their chief officer called Strategos, was chosen in the Congress by a majority of votes. He presided in [45] the Congress, commanded the forces, and was vested with great powers, especially in time of war : but was liable to be called to an account by the Congress, and punished, if convicted of misbehaviour.

The states have been oppressed by the kings of Macedon, and insulted by tyrants. "From their incorporation," says Polybius, "may be dated the birth of that greatness, that by a constant augmentation, at length arrived to a marvellous height of prosperity. The same of their wise laws and mild government reached the Greek colonies in Italy, where the Grotoniates, the Sybarites, and the Cauloniates, agreed to adopt them, and to govern their states conformably."

Did the delegates to the Amphictionic council, or to the Congress of the Achæan league destroy the liberty of their country, by establishing a monarchy or an aristocracy among themselves? Quite the contrary. *While the several states con-*

---

of the confederacy. A body of foot was dispatched who soon occupied the valley of Tempe, the only pass from Lower Macedonia, into Thessaly.

In a few days, these troops being informed that there was another pass from Upper Macedonia, returned to the Corinthian Isthmus.

The Thessalians thus deserted made their submission.

"This retreat from Tempe appears to have been a precipate measure, rendered necessary by nothing so much as by *the want of some powers* of government extending over the several states which composed the confederacy."—Mitford's *History of Greece.*

With diminished forces, the defence of the confederates was now to be contracted. But in the conduct even of this business daily becoming more urgent, we find them laboring under the defects of their confederation.

"Destitute of any sufficient power extending over the whole, no part could confide in the protection of the whole, while the naval superiority of their enemy put it in his choice, where, when, and how to make his attacks : and therefore *tinued faithful to the union, they prospered.*   Their affairs were shattered by dissensions, emulations, and civil wars, artfully and diligently fomented by princes who thought it their interest; and in the case of the Achæan league, partly, by the folly and wickedness of Greeks not of the league, particularly the Ætolians, who repined at the glories, that constantly attended the banner of freedom, supported by virtue and conducted by prudence.   Thus weakened, they all sunk together, the envied and the envying, under the domination, first of Macedon, and then of Rome.

[46] Let any man of common sense peruse the gloomy but instructive pages of their mournful story, and he will be convinced, that if any nation could successfuly have resisted those conquerors of the world, the illustrious deed had been achieved by Greece; that cradle of republics, if the several states had been cemented by some such league as the Achæan, and had honestly fulfilled its obligations.

It is not pretended, that the Achæan league was perfect, or that they were not monarchical and aristocratical factions among the people of it.   Every concession of that sort, that can be asked, shall be made.   It had many defects; every one of which, however, has been avoided in the plan proposed to us.

With all its defects, with all its disorders, yet such was the life and vigor communicated through the whole, by the popular representation of each part, and the close combination of

each republic seems to have been anxious to reserve its own strength for future contingencies.

Their generous hearts all beat at the call of freedom; but their efforts were embarrassed and enfeebled by the vices of their political constitution, to their prodigious detriment, and almost to their total destruction.   For these vices, the ardor of heroism united with love of country could not compensate. These very vices therefore, may truly be said to have wasted the blood of patriots, and to have betrayed their country into the severest calamities.

If *we* shall hereafter by experience discover any vices in our constitution, let us *hasten* with prudence and a fraternal affection for each other, to correct them.   We are all embarked in the same vessel, and equally concerned in repairing any defects.

all, that the true spirit of republicanism *predominated*, and thereby advanced the happiness and glory of the people to so pre-eminent a state that *our* ideas upon the pleasing theme cannot be too elevated. Here is the proof of this assertion. When the Romans had laid Carthage in ashes ; had reduced the kingdom of Macedon to a province ; had conquered Antiochus the great, and got the better of all their enemies in the East ; these Romans, masters of so much of the then known world, determined to humble the Achæan league, because as history expressly informs us, "their great power began to raise no small jealousy at Rome."—Polybius.

[47] What a vast weight of argument do these facts and circumstances add to the maintenance of the principle contended for by the writer of this address?

FABIUS.

LETTER VI.

Some of our fellow-citizens have ventured to predict the future state of United America, if the system proposed to us, shall be adopted.

Though every branch of the constitution and government is to be popular, and guarded by the strongest provisions, that until this day have occurred to mankind, yet the system will end, they say, in the oppressions of a monarchy or aristocracy by the federal servants or some of them.

Such a conclusion seems not in any manner suited to the premises. It startles, yet, not so much from its novelty, as from the respectability of the characters by which it is drawn.

We must not be too much influenced by our esteem for those characters: But, should recollect, that when the fancy is warmed, and the judgment inclined, by the proximity or pressure of particular objects, very extraordinary declarations are not unfrequently made. Such are the frailties of our nature, that genius and integrity sometimes afford no protection against them.

Probably, there never was, and never will be, such an instance of dreadful denunciation, concerning the fate of a country, as was published while the union was in agitation between England and Scotland. The English were for a joint legislature, many of the Scots for separate legislatures, and urged, that they should be in [49] a manner swallowed up and lost in the other, as then they would not possess one eleventh part in it.

Upon that occasion lord Belhaven, one of the most distinguished orators of the age, made in the Scottish parliament a famous speech, of which the following extract is part :

" My lord Chancellor,

" When I consider this affair of an union between the two nations, as it is expressed in the several articles thereof, and now the subject of our deliberation at this time, I find my mind crowded with a variety of very melancholy thoughts, and I think it my duty to disburthen myself of some of them, by laying them before and exposing them to the serious consideration of this honourable house.

"I think, *I see a free and independent kingdom* delivering up that, which all the world hath been fighting for since the days of Nimrod ; yea, that, for which most of all the empires, kingdoms, states, principalities, and dukedoms of Europe, are at this very time engaged in the most bloody and cruel wars that ever were : to wit, *a power to manage their own affairs by themselves, without the assistance aud council of any other.*

"I think I see *a National Church,* founded upon a rock, secured by a claim of right, hedged and fenced about by the strictest and pointedest legal sanctions that sovereignty could contrive, voluntarily descending into a plain upon an equal level with Jews, Paptists, Soci- [50] nians, Armenians, and Anabaptists, and other Sectaries, &c.

"I think I see *the noble and honorable peerage of Scotland,* whose valiant predecessors led against their enemies upon their own proper charges and expences, now divested of their followers and vassalages, and put upon such an equal foot with their vassals, that I think, I see a petty English *exciseman* receive more homage and respect, than what was paid formerly to their quondam Mackallamors.

"I think, I see *the present peers of Scotland,* whose noble ancestors, conquered provinces, over-run countries, reduced and subjected towns and fortified places, exacted tribute through the greatest part of England, now walking in the *court of requests,* like so many English Attornies, laying aside their walking swords when in company with the English Peers, lest their self-defence should be found murder.

"I think, I see *the honorable Estate of Barons,* the bold assertors of the nations rights and liberties in the worst of times, now setting *a watch upon their lips* and *a guard upon their tongues,* lest they be found guilty of *scandalum magnatum.*

"I think I see *the royal State of Boroughs,* walking their *desolate streets,* hanging down their heads *under disappointments ;* worm'd out of *all the branches of their old trade,* uncertain *what hand to turn to,* necessitated to become [51] apprentices to their unkind neighbors, and yet after all finding their *trade so fortified by companies* and secured by prescriptions, that they despair of any success therein.

"I think, I see *our learned Judges* laying aside their practiques and decisions, studying the common law of England, gravelled with certioraries, *nisi priuses*, writs of error, *ejectiones firmæ*, injunctions, demurrers, &c. and frighted with *appeals* and *avocations*, because of *the new regulations*, and *rectifications* they meet with.

"I think, I see *the valiant and gallant soldiery*, either sent to learn the plantation trade abroad, or at home petitioning for *a small subsistence*, as the reward of their honourable exploits, while their old corps are broken, the common soldiers left to beg, and the youngest English corps kept standing.

"I think, I see the *honest industrious tradesman* loaded with *new taxes and impositions*, disappointed of the equivalents, drinking water in place of ale, eating his saltless pottage, petitioning for *encouragement to his manufactories*, and answered by counter petitions.

"In short, I think I see the *laborious ploughman*, with his corn spoiling upon his hands *for want of sale*, cursing the day of his birth; dreading the expence of his burial, and uncertain whether to marry or do worse.

"I think I see the incurable difficulties of *landing men*, fettered under the golden chain of equivalents, their pretty daughters petition- [52] ing for want of husbands, and their sons for want of employments.

"I think I see *our mariners delivering up their ships* to their Dutch partners, and what through *presses and necessity* earning their bread as underlings in the English navy. But above all, my lord, I think, I see *our ancient mother Caledonia*, like Cæsar, sitting in the midst of our senate, ruefully looking round about her, covering herself with her royal garment, attending the fatal blows and breathing out her last with a ———*Et tu quoque mi fili.*

"Are not these, my lord, very afflicting thoughts? And yet they are the least part suggested to me by these dishonorable articles. Should not the considerations of these things

vivify these dry bones of ours? Should not the memory of
our noble predecessors' valor and constancy rouse up our
drooping spirits? Are our noble predecessors' souls got so far
into the English cabbage-stalks and cauliflowers, that we
should shew the least inclination that way? Are our eyes so
blinded? Are our ears so deafened? Are our hearts so hard-
ened? Are our tongues so faultered? Are our hands so fettered? that in this our day, I say, my lord, that in this our
day, we should not mind the things that concern the very
being and well being of our ancient kingdom, before the day
be hid from our eyes.

"When I consider this treaty as it hath been explained,
and spoke to, before us these three weeks by past; I see the
English constitution remaining firm, the same *two houses* of
Par- [53] liament, the same *taxes*, the same *customs*, the same
excises, the same *trading companies*, the same municipal laws
and courts of judicature; *and all ours either subject to regulations or annihilations*, only we are to have *the honor* to pay
their old debts, and to have some few persons present for wit-
nesses, to the validity of the deed, when they are pleased to
contract more."*

Let any candid American deliberately compare that trans-
action with the present, and laying his hand upon his heart,
solemnly answer this question to himself—Whether, he does
not verily believe the eloquent Peer before mentioned, had
ten-fold more cause to apprehend evils from such an unequal
match between the two kingdoms, that any citizen of these
states has to apprehend them from the system proposed?
Indeed not only that Peer, but other persons of distinction,
and large numbers of the people of Scotland were filled with
the utmost aversion to the union; and if the greatest diligence
and prudence had not been employed by its friends in remov-
ing misapprehensions and refuting misrepresentations, and by
the then subsisting government for preserving the public
peace, there would certainly have been a rebellion.

Yet, *what were the consequences* to Scotland of that *dreaded*

---

* See objections against the Federal constitution, very similar to those
made in Scotland.

union with England? The cultivation of her virtues and the correction of her errors—The emancipation of one [54] class of her citizens from the yoke of her superiors—A relief of other classes from the injuries and insults of the great—Improvements in agriculture, science, arts, trade, and manufactures—The profits of industry and ingenuity enjoyed under the protection of laws—peace and security at home, and encrease of respectability abroad. Her Church is still eminent —Her laws and courts of judicature are safe—Her boroughs grown into cities—Her mariners and soldiery possessing a larger subsistence than she could have afforded them, and her tradesmen, ploughmen, landed men, and her people of every rank, in a more flourishing condition, not only than they ever were, but in a more flourishing condition, than the clearest understanding could, at the time, have thought it possible for them to attain in so short a period, or even in many ages. England participated in the blessings. The stock of their union or ingraftment, as perhaps it may be called, being strong and capable of drawing better nutriment and in greater abundance, than they could ever have done apart,

"Ere long, to Heaven the soaring branches shoot,
"And wonder at their height, and more than native fruit."

FABIUS.

[55]   LETTER VII.

Thus happily mistaken was the ingenious, learned, and patriotic lord Belhaven, in his prediction concerning the fate of his country; and thus happily mistaken, it is hoped, some of our fellow-citizens will be, in their prediction concerning the fate of their country.

Had they taken large scope, and assumed in their proposition the vicissitude of human affairs, and the passions that so often confound them, their prediction might have been a tolerably good guess. Amidst the mutabilities of terrestrial things, the liberty of United America may be destroyed. As to that point, it is our duty, humbly, constantly, fervently, to implore the protection of our most gracious maker, "who doth not afflict willingly nor grieve the children of men," and incessantly to strive, as we are commanded, to recommend ourselves to that protection, by "doing his will," diligently exercising our reason in fulfilling the purposes for which that and our existence were given to us.

How the liberty of this country is to be destroyed, is another question. Here, the gentlemen assign a cause, in no manner proportioned, as it is apprehended, to the effect.

The uniform tenor of history is against them. That holds up the *licentiousness* of the people, and *turbulent temper* of some of the states, as *the only causes* to be dreaded, not the conspiracies of federal officers. There-[56]fore, it is highly probable, that, if our liberty is ever subverted, it will be by one of the two causes first mentioned. Our tragedy will then have the same acts, with those of the nations that have gone before us; and we shall add one more example to the number already too great, of people that would not take warning, not, "know the things which belong to their peace." But, we ought not to pass such a sentence against our country, and the interests of freedom: Though, no sentence whatever can be equal to the atrocity of our guilt, if through enormity of obstinacy or baseness, we betray the cause of our posterity and of mankind, by providence committed to our parental and fraternal care.

There is reason to believe, that the calamities of nations are the punishments of their sins.

As to the first mentioned cause, it seems unnecssary to say any more upon it.

As to the second, we find, that the misbehaviour of the constituent parts acting separately, or in partial confederacies, debilitated the Greeks under The Amphictionic Council, and under The Achæan League. As to the former, it was not entirely an assembly of strictly democratical republics. Besides, it wanted a sufficiently close connection of its parts. After these observations, we may call our attention from it.

'Tis true, The Achæan League was disturbed by the misconduct of some parts, but it is as true, that it surmounted these difficulties, and wonderfully prospered, until it was dissolved in the manner that has been described.

[57] The glorious operations of its principles bear the clearest testimony to this distant age and people, that the wit of man never invented such an antidote against monarchical and aristocratical projects, as a strong combination of truly democratical republics. By strictly or truly democratical republics, the writer means republics in which all the principal officers, except the judicial, are from time to time chosen by the people.

The reason is plain. As liberty and equality, or as well termed by Polybius, *benignity*, were the foundations of their institutions, and the energy of the government pervaded all the parts in things relating to the whole, it counteracted for the common welfare, the designs hatched by selfishness in separate councils.

If folly or wickedness prevailed in any parts, friendly offices and salutary measures restored tranquility. Thus the public good was maintained. In its very formation, tyrannies and aristocracies submitted, by consent or compulsion. Thus, the Ceraunians, Trezenians, Epidaurians, Megalopolitans, Argives, Hermionians, and Phlyayzrians were received into the league. A happy exchange! For history informs us, that so true were they to their noble and benevolent principles, that, in their diet, " *no resolutions were taken, but what were equally*

*advantageous to the whole confederacy, and the interest of each
part so consulted, as to leave no room for complaints !"*

[58] How degrading would be the thought to a citizen of
United America, that the people of these states, with institutions beyond comparison preferable to those of The Achæan
league, and so vast a superiority in other respects, should not
have wisdom and virtue enough, to manage their affairs, with
as much prudence and affection of one for another as these
ancients did.

Would this be doing justice to our country? The composition of her temper is excellent, and seems to be acknowl-
edged equal to that of any nation in the world. Her prudence
will guard its warmth against two faults, to which it may be
exposed—The one, an imitation of *foreign fashions*, which
from small things may lead to great. May her citizens aspire
at a national dignity in every part of conduct, private as well
as public. This will be influenced by the former. May *sim-
plicity* be the characteristic feature of their manners, which,
inlaid with their other virtues and their forms of government,
may then indeed be compared, in the Eastern stile, to "apples
of gold in pictures of silver." Thus will they long, and may
they, while their rivers run, escape the contagion of luxury—
that motley issue of innocence debauched by folly, and the
lineal predecessor of tyranny, prolific of guilt and wretched-
ness. The other fault, of which, as yet, there are no symptoms
among us, is the *thirst of empire*. This is a vice, that ever has
been, and from the nature of things, ever must be, fatal to republican [59] forms of government. Our wants, are sources
of happiness: our irregular desires, of misery. The abuse of
prosperity, is rebellion against Heaven; and succeeds accord-
ingly.

Do the propositions of gentlemen who object, offer to our
view, any of *the great points* upon which, the fate, fame, or
freedom of nations has turned, excepting what some of them
have said about trial by jury; and which has been frequently
and fully answered? Is there one of them calculated to regulate, and if needful, to *controul* those tempers and measures of
constituent parts of an union, that have been so baneful to the

weal of every confederacy that has existed? Do not some of them tend to enervate the authority evidently designed thus to regulate and controul? Do not others of them discover a bias in their advocates to particular connections, that if indulged to them, would enable persons of less understanding and virtue, to repeat the disorders, that have so often violated public peace and honor? Taking them altogether, would they afford as strong a security to our liberty, as the frequent election of the federal officers by the people, and the repartition of power among those officers, according to the proposed system?

It may be answered, that, they would be an additional security. In reply, let the writer be permitted at present to refer to what has been said.

The principal argument of gentlemen who object, involves a direct proof of the point contended for by the writer of this address, and as [60] far as it may be supposed to be founded, a plain confirmation of Historic evidence.

They generally agree, that the great danger of a monarchy or aristocracy among us, will arise from the federal senate.

The members of this senate, are to be chosen by men exercising the sovereignty of their respective states. These men therefore must be monarchically or aristocratically disposed, before they will chuse federal senators thus disposed ; and what merits particular attention, is, that these men must have obtained an overbearing influence in their respective states, before they could with such disposition arrive at the exercise of the sovereignty in them : or else, the like disposition must be prevalent among the people of such states.

Taking the case either way, is not this a disorder in parts of the union, and ought it not to be rectified by the rest? Is it reasonable to expect, that the disease will seize all at the same time? If it is not, ought not the sound to possess a right and power, by which they may prevent the infection from spreading? And will not *the extent* of our territory, and the *number* of states within it, vastly increase the difficulty of any political disorder diffusing its contagion, and the probability of its being repressed?

From the annals of mankind, these conclusions are deducible—that confederated states may act prudently and honestly, and apart foolishly and knavishly ; but, that it is a defiance [61] of all probability, to suppose, that states conjointly shall act with folly and wickedness, and yet separately with wisdom and virtue.

FABIUS.

---

[62]   LETTER VIII.

The proposed confederation offers to us a system of diversified representation in the legislative, executive, and judicial departments, as essentially necessary to the good government of an extensive republican empire. Every argument to recommend it, receives new force, by contemplating events, that must take place. The number of states in America will increase. If not united to the present, the consequences are evident. If united, it must be by a plan that will communicate equal liberty and assure just protection to them. These ends can never be attained, but by a close combination of the several states.

It has been asserted, that a very extensive territory cannot be ruled by a government of republican form. What is meant by this proposition ? Is it intended to abolish all ideas of connection, and to precipitate us into the miseries of division, either as single states, or partial confederacies ? To stupify us into despondence, that destruction may certainly seize us ? The fancy of poets never feigned so dire a Metamorphosis, as is now held up to us. The Ægis of their Minerva was only said to turn men into stones. This spell is to turn " a band of brethren," into a monster, preying on itself, and preyed upon by all its enemies.

If hope is not to be abandoned, common sense teaches us to attempt the best means of preservation. This is all that men can do, and [63] this they ought to do. Will it be said, that any kind of disunion, or a connection tending to it, is preferable to a firm union? Or, is there any charm in that despotism, which is said, to be alone competent to the rule of such an empire? There is no evidence of fact, nor any deduction of reason, that justifies the assertion. It is true, that extensive territory has in general been arbitrarily governed; and it is as true, that a number of republics, in such territory, loosely connected, must inevitably rot into despotism.

It is said—Such territory has never been governed by a confederacy of republics. Granted. But, where was there ever a confederacy of republics, in such territory, united, as these states are to be by the proposed constitution? Where was there ever a confederacy, in which, the sovereignty of each state was equally represented in one legislative body, the people of each state equally represented in another, and the sovereignties and people of all the states conjointly represented, possessed such a qualified and temperating authority in making laws? Or, in which the appointment to federal offices was vested in a chief magistrate chosen as our president is to be? Or, in which, the acts of the executive department were regulated, as they are to be with us? Or, in which, the federal judges were to hold their offices independently and during good behaviour? Or, in which, the authority over the militia and troops was so distributed and controuled, as it is to be with us? Or, in which, the people were so drawn together by religion, blood, language, manners and [64] customs, undisturbed by former feuds or prejudices? Or, in which, the affairs relating to the whole union, were to be managed by an assembly of several representative bodies, invested with different powers that became efficient only in concert, without their being embarrassed by attention to other business? Or, in which, a provision was made for the federal revenue, without recurring to coercion against states, the miserable expedient, of every other confederacy that has existed, an expedient always attended with odium, and often with a delay productive of irreparable damage? Where was there ever a confederacy, that thus adhered to the first principle in civil society ; obliging by its direct authority every individual, to contribute, when the public good necessarily required it, a just proportion of aid to the support of the commonwealth protecting him—without disturbing him in the discharge of the duties owing by him to the state of which he is an inhabitant; and at the same time, so amply, so anxiously provided, for bringing the interests, and even the wishes of every sovereignty and of every person of the union, under all their various modifications and impressions, into their full operation and efficacy in the national councils? The instance never existed. The conclusion ought not to be made. It is without premises. So far is the assertion from being true, that " a very extensive territory cannot be ruled by a government of a republican form," that such a territory cannot be well-ruled by a government of any other form.

[65] The assertion has probably been suggested by reflections on the democracies of antiquity, without making a proper distinction between them and the democracy of The United States.

In the democracies of antiquity, the people assembled together and governed personally. This mode was incompatible with greatness of number and dispersion of habitation.

In the democracy of The United States, the people act by their representatives. This improvement collects the will of millions upon points concerning their welfare, with more advantage, than the will of hundreds could be collected under the ancient form.

There is another improvement equally deserving regard, and that is, the varied representation of sovereignties and people in the constitution now proposed.

It has been said, that this representation was a mere compromise.

It was not a mere compromise. *The equal representation of each state in one branch of the legislature*, was an original substantive proposition, made in convention, very soon after the draft offered by Virginia, to which last mentioned state United America is much indebted not only in other respects, but for her merit in the origination and prosecution of this momentous business.

The proposition was expressly made upon this principle, that a territory of such extent as that of United America, could not be safely and advantageously governed, but by a combination of republics, each retaining all the rights of supreme [66] sovereignty, excepting such as ought to be contributed to the union; that for the securer preservation of these sovereignties, they ought to be represented in a body by themselves, and with equal suffrage ; and that they would be annihilated, if both branches of the legislature were to be formed of representatives of the people, in proportion to the number of inhabitants in each state.*

The principle appears to be well founded in reason,   Why cannot a very extensive territory be ruled by a government of republican form ? They answered, because its power must languish through distance of parts. Granted, if it be not a "body by joints and bands having nourishment ministered and knit together." If it be such a body, the objection is removed. Instead of such a perfect body, framed upon the principle that commands men to associate, and societies to confederate ; that, which by communicating and extending happiness, corresponds with the gracious intentions of our maker towards us his creatures? what is proposed? Truly, that the natural legs and arms of this body should be cut off, because they are too weak, and their places supplied by strongest limbs of wood and metal.

[67] Monarchs, it is said, are enabled to rule extensive territories. because they send viceroys to govern certain districts ; and thus the reigning authority is transmitted over the whole empire. Be it so : But what are the consequences? Tyranny, while the viceroys continue in submission to their masters, and the distraction of civil war besides, when they revolt, to which they are frequently tempted by the very circumstances of their situation, as the history of such governments indisputably proves.

* Justice Blackstone argues in like manner, after admitting the "expediency" of titles of nobility. "It is also expedient that their owners should form an independent and separate branch of the legislature"—otherwise "their privileges would soon be borne down and overwhelmed."—Comment. 2. 157.

America is, and will be, divided into several sovereign states, each possessing every power proper for governing within its own limits for its own purposes, and also for acting as a member of the union.

They will be civil and military stations, conveniently planted throughout the empire, with lively and regular communications. A stroke, a touch upon any part, will be immediately felt by the whole. Rome famed for imperial arts, had a glimpse of this great truth; and endeavoured, as well as her hard-hearted policy would permit, to realize it in her *colonies*. They were miniatures of the capital: But wanted the vital principal of sovereignty, and were too small. They were melted down into, or overwhelmed by the nations around them. Were they now existing, they might be called curious automatons—something like to our living originals. These, will bear a remarkable resemblance to the mild features of patriarchal government, in which each son ruled his own household, and in other matters the whole family was directed by the common ancestor.

[68] Will a people thus happily situated, ever desire to exchange their condition, for subjection to an absolute ruler; or can they ever look but with veneration, or act but with deference to that union, that alone can, under providence, preserve them from such subjugation?

Can any government be devised, that will be more suited to citizens, who wish for equal freedom and common prosperity; better calculated for preventing corruption of manners; for advancing the improvements that endear or adorn life; or that can be more conformed to the understanding, to the best affections, to the very nature of *man*? What harvests of happiness may grow from the seeds of liberty that are now sowing? The cultivation will indeed demand continual attention, unceasing diligence, and frequent conflict with difficulties: but, to object against the benefits offered to us by our Creator, by excepting to the terms annexed, is a crime to be equalled only by its folly.

Delightful are the prospects that will open to the view of United America—her sons well prepared to defend their own happiness, and ready to relieve the misery of others—her fleets formidable, but only to the unjust—her revenue sufficient, yet unoppressive—her commerce affluent, but not debasing—peace and plenty within her borders—and the glory that arises from a proper use of power, encircling them.

Whatever regions may be destined for servitude, let us hope, that some portions of this land may be blessed with liberty; let us be con- [69] vinced, that *nothing short of such an union* as has been proposed, can preserve the blessing; and therefore let us be resolved to adopt it.

As to alterations, a little *experience* will cast more light upon the subject, than a multitude of debates. Whatever qualities are possessed by those who object, they will have the candor to confess, that they will be encountered by opponents, not in any respect inferior, and yet differing from them in judgment, upon every point they have mentioned.

Such untired industry to serve their country, did the delegates to the federal convention exert, that they not only laboured to form the best plan they could, but, *provided for making at any time amendments on the authority of the people*, without shaking the stability of the government. For this end, the Congress, whenever two-thirds of both houses shall deem it necessary, shall propose amendments to the constitution, or, on the application of the legislatures of two-thirds of the several states, *shall* call a convention for proposing amendments, which, in either case, shall be valid to all intents and purposes, as part of the constitution, when ratified by the legislatures of three-fourths of the several states, or by conventions in three-fourths thereof, as one or the other mode of ratification may be proposed by Congress.

Thus, by a gradual progress, we may from time to time *introduce every improvement in our constitution*, that shall be [70] suitable to our situation. For this purpose, it may perhaps be advisable, for every state, as it sees occasion, to form with the utmost deliberation, drafts of alterations respectively required by them, and to enjoin their representatives, to employ every proper method to obtain a ratification.

In this way of proceeding, the undoubted sense of every

state, collected in the coolest manner, not the sense of individuals, will be laid before the whole union in congress, and that body will be enabled with the clearest light that can be afforded by every part of it, and with the least occasion of irritation, to compare and weigh the sentiments of all United America; forthwith to adopt such alterations as are recommended by general unanimity; by degrees to devise modes of conciliation upon contradictory propositions; and to give the revered advice of our common country, upon those, if any such there should be, that in her judgment are inadmissible, because they are incompatible with the happiness of these states.

It cannot be with reason apprehended, that Congress will refuse to act upon any articles calculated to promote the *common* welfare, though they may be unwilling to act upon such as are designed to advance *partial* interests : but, whatever their sentiments may be, they *must* call a convention for proposing amendments, on applications of two-thirds of the legislatures of the several states.

May those good citizens, who have sometimes turned their thoughts towards a second [71] convention, be pleased to consider, that there are men who speak as they do, yet do not mean as they do. These borrow the sanction of their respected names, to conceal desperate designs. May they also consider, whether persisting in the suggested plan, in preference to the constitutional provision, may not kindle flames of jealousy and discord, which all their abilities and virtues can never extinguish.

FABIUS.

[72]   LETTER IX.

When the sentiments of some objectors, concerning the British constitution, are considered, it is surprising, that they should apprehend so much danger to United America, as, they say, will attend the ratification of the plan proposed to us, by the late federal convention.

These gentlemen will acknowledge, that Britain has sustained many internal convulsions, and many foreign wars, with a gradual advancement in freedom, power, and prosperity. They will acknowledge, that no nation has existed that ever so perfectly united those distant extremes, private security of life, liberty, and property, with exertion of public force—so advantageously combined the various powers of militia, troops, and fleets—or so happily blended together arms, arts, science, commerce, and agriculture. From what spring has flowed this stream of happiness? The gentlemen will acknowledge, that these advantages are derived from a single democratical branch in her legislature. They will also acknowledge, that in this branch, called the house of commons, only one hundred and thirty-one are members for counties : that nearly one half of the whole house is chosen by about five thousand seven hundred persons, mostly of no property ; that fifty-six members are elected by about three hundred and seventy [73] persons, and the rest in an enormous disproportion* to the numbers of inhabitants who ought to vote.†

Thus are all the millions of people in that kingdom, said to be represented in the house of commons.

Let the gentlemen be so good, on a subject so familiar to them, as to make a comparison between the British constitution, and that proposed to us. Questions like these will then

* No member of parliament ought to be elected by fewer than the majority of 800, upon the most moderate calculation, according to Doctor Price.

† By the constitution proposed to us, a majority of the house of representatives, and of the senate, makes a quorum to do business : but, if the writer is not mistaken, about a fourteenth part of the members of the house of commons, makes a quorum for that purpose.

probably present themselves : Is there more danger to our liberty, from such a president as we are to have, than to that of Britons from an hereditary monarch with a vast revenue— absolute in the erection and disposal of offices, and in the ex- ercise of the whole executive power—in the command of the militia, fleets, and armies, and the direction of their operations —in the establishments of fairs and markets, the regulation of weights and measures, and coining of money—who can call parliaments with a breath, and dissolve them with a nod—who can, at his will, make war, peace, and treaties irrevocably bind- ing the nation—and who can [74] grant pardons and titles of nobility, as it pleases him ? Is there more danger to us, from twenty-six senators, or double the number, than to Britons, from an hereditary aristocratic body, consisting of many hun- dreds, possessed of enormous wealth in lands and money— strengthened by a host of dependants—and who, availing themselves of defects in the constitution, send many of these into the house of commons—who hold a third part of the legislative power in their own hands—and who form the highest court of judicature in the nation ? Is there more dan- ger to us, from a house of representatives, to be chosen by all the freemen of the union, every two years, than to Britons, from such a sort of representation as they have in the house of commons, the members of which, too, are chosen but every seven years ? Is there more danger to us, from the intended federal officers, than to Britons, from such a monarch, aristo- cracy, and house of commons together ? *What bodies* are there in Britain, vested with such capacities for enquiring into, checking, and regulating the conduct of national affairs, *as our sovereign states ?* What proportion does the number of *free holders* in Britain bear to the number of people ? And what is the proportion in United America ?

If any person, after considering such questions, shall say, there will be more danger to our freedom under the proposed plan, than to that of Britons under their constitution, he must mean, that Americans are, or will be, beyond all comparison, inferior to Britons in under- [75] standing and virtue ; other- wise, with a constitution and government, every branch of which is so extremely popular, they certainly might guard their rights, at least at well, as Britons can guard theirs, under such political institutions as they have; unless the person has some inclination to an opinion, that monarchy and aristocracy are favourable to the preservation of their rights. If he has, he cannot too soon recover himself. If ever monarchy or aristocracy appears in this country, in must be in the hideous form of despotism.

What an infatuated, depraved people must Americans become, if, with such unequalled advantages, committed to their trust in a manner almost miraculous, they lose their liberty? Through a single organ of representation, in the legislature only, of the kingdom just mentioned, though that organ is diseased, such portions of popular sense and integrity have been conveyed into the national councils, as have purified other parts, and preserved the whole in its present state of healthfulness. To their own vigour and attention, therefore, is that people, under providence, indebted for the blessings they enjoy. They have held, and now hold *the true balance* in their government. While they retain their enlightened spirit, they will continue to hold it; and *if they regard what they owe to others*, as well as what they owe to themselves, they will, most probably, continue to be happy.*

[76] They know, that there are powers that cannot be expressly limited, without injury to themselves; and their mag-

---

* If to the union of England and Scotland, a just connection with Ireland be added, ecclesiastical establishments duly amended ; additions to the peerage regulated, and representation of the commons properly improved, it is to be expected, that the tranquility, strength, reputation, and prosperity of the empire will be greatly promoted, the monarchy will probably change into a republic, if representation in the house of commons is not encreased by additions from the counties and great trading cities and towns, without this precaution, an increase of the peerage seems likely to accelerate an alteration. These two measures should have. it is apprehended, in such a government and in such a progress of human affairs, a well-tempered co-operation. The power of the crown might thereby become more dignified, moderated, and secured.

The discussion of this subject would embrace a very great number of considerations ; but the conclusion seems to approach as near to demonstration, as an investigation of this kind can do.

nanimity scorns any fear of such powers. This magnanimity taught Charles the first, that he was but a royal servant; and this magnanimity caused James the second's army, raised, paid, and kept up by himself, to confound him with huzzas for liberty.

They ask not for compacts, of which the national welfare, and, in some cases, its existence, may demand violations. They despise such dangerous provisions against danger.

They know, that all powers whatever, even those that, according to the forms of the con- [77] stitution, are irresistible and absolute, of which there are many, ought to be exercised for the public good; and that when they are used to the public detriment, they are unconstitutionally exerted.

This plain text, commented upon by their experienced intelligence, has led them safe through hazards of every kind: and they now are, what we see them. Upon the review, one is almost tempted to believe, that their insular situation, soil, climate, and some other circumstances, have compounded a peculiarity of temperature, uncommonly favourable to the union of reason and passion.

Certainly, 'tis very memorable, with what life, impartiality, and prudence, they have interposed on great occasions; have by their patriotism communicated temporary soundness to their disordered representation; and have bid public confusions to cease. Two instances out of many may suffice. The excellent William the third was distressed by a house of commons. He dissolved the parliament, and appealed to the people. They relieved him. His successor, the present king, in the like distress, made the same appeal; and received equal relief.

Thus they have acted: but Americans, who have the same blood in their veins, have, it seems, very different heads and hearts. We shall be enslaved by a president, senators, and representatives, chosen by ourselves, and continually rotating within the period of time assigned for the continuance in office of members in the house of commons? 'Tis strange: but, we are told, 'tis true. It may be so. As we [78] have our all at stake, let us enquire, in what way this event is to

be brought about.   Is it to be before or after a general corruption of manners?   If after, it is not worth attention.   The
loss of happiness then follows of course.   If before, how is it
to be accomplished?   Will a virtuous and sensible people
choose villains or fools for their officers?   Or, if they should
choose men of wisdom and integrity, will these lose both or
either, by taking their seats?   If they should, will not their places
be quickly supplied by another choice?   Is the like derangement again, and again, and again, to be expected?   Can any
man believe, that such astonishing phænomena are to be looked
for?   Was there ever an instance, where rulers, thus selected
by the people from their own body, have, in the manner apprehended, outraged their own tender connexions, and the interests, feelings, and sentiments of their affectionate and con-
fiding countrymen?   Is such a conduct more likely to prevail
in this age of mankind, than in the darker periods that have
preceded?   Are men more disposed now than formerly,
to prefer uncertainties to certainties, things perilous and infamous to those that are safe and honorable?   Can all the
mysteries of such iniquity, be so wonderfully managed by
treacherous rulers, that none of their enlightened constitu-
ents, nor any of their honest associates, acting with them in
public bodies, shall ever be able to discover the conspiracy,
till at last it shall burst with destruction to the whole federal
constitution?   Is it not ten thousand times less probable, that
such [79] transactions will happen, than it is, that we shall be
exposed to innumerable calamities, by rejecting the plan proposed, or even by delaying to accept it?

Let us consider our affairs in another light.   Our differ-
ence of government, participation in commerce, improvement
in policy, and magnitude of power, can be no favourite objects
of attention to the Monarchies and Sovereignties of Europe.
Our loss will be their gain—our fall, their rise—our shame,
their triumph.   Divided, they may distract, dictate, and
destroy.   United, their efforts will be waves dashing themselves into foam against a rock.   May our national character
be—an animated moderation, that seeks only its own, and will
not be satisfied with less.

To his beloved fellow-citizens of United America, the writer dedicates this imperfect testimony of his affection, with fervent prayers, for a perpetuity of freedom, virtue, piety, and felicity, to them and their posterity.

F A B I U S.